GIVE A SH*T!

How to Recruit, Select, and Hire Extraordinary Talent

By

Dean Hohl

Army Ranger, Corporate HR Manager & Entrepreneur

Published by:
RealTime Publishing
Limerick, Ireland
ISBN: 978-1-84961-166-4

DEDICATION

This book is dedicated to the frontline supervisors and managers with the grit determination to lead and succeed on today's complex "Business Battlefield!" Lead The Way!

TABLE OF CONTENTS

PART TWO: WINNING WITH THE "HIRE FOR LIFE" ORGANIZATION

Chapter Four: Great Expectations.

Basic hiring procedures.

Rules of the road: The framework of rules that will allow you to apply the selection process objectively and with the highest possible standards.

Chapter Five: The Competitive Advantages "Hire for Life" Provides.

Chapter Six: Recruiting Channels: Where it Works and where It Doesn't.

Defining the "right" job candidate.

Recruiters and Headhunters: The good, the bad, and the ugly.

The problem with traditional print ads.

Online job boards.

Social networking websites.

Referrals.

What's best for you?

Chapter Seven: Assessing Job Candidates.

Third party assessment tools.

Step 5: Appraise the candidate pool.

Step 6: Make the final decision.

Step 7: Conduct post-hire introductions, orientation and follow-up.

Chapter Twelve: Summary

Focus on the RASI process.

GAS Gauge questions.

Appendix: Ready to use GAS Gauge Diagram

PART ONE

WHY TRADITIONAL HIRING TACTICS
FAIL THE ORGANIZATION

CHAPTER ONE
THE SAD (AND UNNECESSARY)
FAILURE OF MARCO Z

Marco Z was ecstatic. Not only had the vice president of manufacturing promoted him to supervisor of his department, he had also granted Marco full hiring and training responsibility for the workers he now supervised.

Quite a responsibility for a young man who had hired on with his company right out of high school and over the course of five years steadily advanced from assistant machine operator to machine operator, then to machine setup specialist, and finally to supervisor.

In all of the steps leading up to Marco's promotion to management rank his duties had been technical; Marco's former supervisor had handled all management issues including decisions regarding hiring, disciplining, and firing.

Such a bright future, but within a year Marco was teetering on the brink of failure; the three workers he had hired within his first ten months as a supervisor were outright disasters: the first was lazy, the second a troublemaker, and the third looked okay but quit after sixty days on the job. Marco justifiably fired the first two.

Needless to say, Marco's boss was not happy. The constant hiring and firing and disruption it caused had dragged down the productivity of Marco's section. To make matters worse, scrap and rejects were at an all-time high.

How did Marco get in this mess, and what lesson does it provide for the rest of us? Let's start with Marco's first hire.

Before contacting Human Resources to locate viable candidates, Marco asked his boss Frank, the department manager, for advice:

"Frank, what's the best way to go about choosing the best person for the job opening?"

Frank pondered the question. "The best advice I can give you, Marco, is the same I received from my boss when I first became a supervisor . . . oh so many years ago."

Marco smiles. "C'mon, Frank, you're still a young man." Marco is nothing if not an adroit political player.

"The best—let me correct that—the only way to find out if the guy you hire is going to cut the mustard, is to have HR[1] select the best candidate possible, then throw him into the job and see how well he performs."

"Sort of sink or swim, eh?"

"Exactly. Trial by fire is another way to put it. The tougher candidate will be able to handle everything you throw at him. That's the kind of guy that makes the best employee."

Marco had his doubts, but he was in no position to ignore his boss' advice. So he did as the boss suggested, and three months later Marco fired the new employee for slacking off on the job. A troubling start to say the least for Marco.

For his next hire, Marco consulted the HR representative, a savvy young woman with an MBA from an Ivy League school. He asked her how to select the best job candidate to replace the employee he just fired.

"That's simple, Marco. I have a book that will help you screen and select job candidates." She pulled out a large tome from the bookcase behind her, thumbed through the pages until she reached the spot she wanted, and handed the book to Marco. "Read those few pages and you'll discover the secret to effective hiring."

---

[1] Human Resources

Marco obediently thumbed through the pages. He read advice such as:

Know what you're looking for
Screen out all but three candidates
Treat them all equally
Check the candidates' references
Hire the best candidate possible

After reading those vague hiring nostrums and others like them, Marco was more confused than ever. Still he tried to assimilate all of the (often contradictory) hiring principles laid down in the book, even though he was gun shy from the last piece of bad hiring advice he received from his boss.

Unfortunately, Marco struck out again. The new employee turned out to be a troublemaker and Marco had to fire him.

Now thoroughly frustrated, Marco turned to his uncle, a recruiter for a national firm. His uncle advised using personality testing which, he claimed, can sort the good guys from the bad guys. Coincidentally, Marco's company had been experimenting with personality testing, and its HR manager was eager to try out the new method.

HR conducted extensive personality testing on the replacement job candidates and relied on the test exclusively to make a hiring decision. Sixty days later, the new employee quit.

To make matters worse, even the two new machine operators hired by Marco's predecessor the past year were turning in lackluster performances. His boss had had high expectations from both; although their work was satisfactory, it wasn't anywhere near outstanding. Not the kind of performance you'd want to build a future on.

And Marco was catching hell for it. His boss was losing patience and considering demoting or firing Marco.

It didn't have to be this way. I'm going to show you in later how Marco could have excelled at hiring the best possible employees and solidify his standing with upper management.

How My Training Turns Wannabes into Hiring Stars

My name is Dean Hohl. I have been leading teams and coaching individuals professionally since 1993. From 1988 to 1992 I served with 3rd Ranger Battalion and helped in the removal of Manuel Noriega when I parachuted onto a hostile Panamanian airstrip.

I graduated Ranger school with honors, earning one of two distinguished "Merrill's Marauders" awards, received only by two Rangers for each class. My peer group chose me for demonstrating exceptional teamwork, leadership, and communication skills under long periods of stress and pressure—often the result of days without food or sleep, throughout the entire 72 day course. I completed my Ranger service with honor at the rank of sergeant.

Since leaving the Rangers in '92 I've held the following roles:

- Co-founder and President: Leading Concepts Team Leadership Institute. Modeled after Ranger school but tailored to meet corporate audiences, Leading Concepts delivers real leadership and team building experiences that help improve bottom line results on the business battlefield.

- Co-author of *Rangers Lead The Way: The Army Rangers' Guide To Leading Your Organization Through Chaos*. This book was favorably reviewed in the *New York Times, Fortune, Bloomberg,* and *Fast Company*.

- Director of Human Resources & Training for a tier one automotive supplier with 700+ associates.

- Global HR manager for a $500MM electronics company with 3500+ associates.

This background has prepared me for the rigors of battle in today's fierce business environment, an environment in which hiring for life provides an enormous competitive advantage.

Now read on and discover the breakthrough in hiring that rescued Marco (you'll learn his fate in Chapter Three), a method that can help you hire and retain the best possible employees for life. Why settle for less?

CHAPTER TWO
THE STAGGERING COST
OF EMPLOYEE TURNOVER

According to many sources[2] *the cost of losing and rehiring employees ranges from 30 to 50 percent of the annual salary of entry-level employees, 150 percent of middle level employees, and up to 400 percent for specialized, high level employees.* Those numbers are sky-high and provide an insight into the truly staggering cost of employee turnover.

The Bureau of Labor Statistics[3] reports that the average private company worker in June, 2011 received a base pay of $19.81 per hour and a benefit package of $8.32 per hour for an hourly total of $28.13, or an annual total of $58, 510.40.

Now, assuming the cost of turnover is equivalent to an average of 100 percent of total pay (a reasonable estimate for a range of employees from worker to executive suite), if the typical small to midsized company of 100 employees loses and replaces seven people annually, then the cost of turnover for the year is:

$58,510.40 x 2 x 7 = $819, 145.60 bottom line cost.

Now further assuming the company's profit margin is 10 percent, then *it needs $8,191, 450 in additional revenue (10 x $819, 145.60) to compensate for lost profits due to employee turnover.* How

[2] One of them the Samenmais Corporations. See
http://www.samenmais.com/articles.php?action=art&aid=6
[3] http://www.bls.gov/news.release/ecec.nr0.htm

many small to mid-sized companies that you know of can generate such revenue, particularly in today's stagnant economy? You're right: very few. Meaning that profits will shrink and the company may even lose money for the year. When high turnover persists from year to year both profits and morale erode and the company's competitive position erodes with it.

Objective and Subjective Losses

You just read an example of objective losses. A definition of objective losses is losses that are measureable such as inventory turnover rates, overtime, production losses, warranty cost, and missed schedules.

Subjective losses are more difficult to quantify. These include low morale, burnout (for those left to carry the workload during employee vacancies), and stagnation (employees are unable to grow if they're still covering vacated jobs). The cumulative result of these translates into higher costs, lower profits, and lost customers because of poor quality.

Let's examine a few of the more devastating turnover costs and their affect on organizations:

Marginalized employee performance: This is the most insidious of turnover costs. Marginal employees are productive enough to get by, but not productive enough to excel. This translates into lower productivity and quality, so-so customer service, s-l-o-w resolution of problems, excessive training costs, and marginalization of every other category of employee performance. Safety also takes a hit because marginal employees have the tendency to take short cuts that result in injuries. Keep enough such employees on the payroll and company performance will sink. Marginal companies composed of marginal employees cannot consistently meet profit expectations, nor can they flourish in today's cutthroat economy where the competition is intense.

Lost sales: When salespeople leave the company, panic often ensues, especially when the company's sales performance is already lagging. The pressure to achieve monthly, quarterly, and annual goals is so intense that top management often succumbs to the pressure and drops a body (any warm body) into the vacant job, crosses their fingers, and hopes for the best. The inevitable result is lost sales and lost market share.

Low morale: When an organization is not fully staffed or some of its staff is not up to the competence level of the rest, low morale predominates. Look at it this way: Say you're a machine operator working in an assembly operation and the person feeding you work upstream is incapable or not motivated to keep you supplied with a steady stream of parts. If your incentive pay is based on the number of quality parts you produce, you're going to feel angry and frustrated. If the situation doesn't improve your morale is going to drop off the charts. Eventually you'll quit and go with another company that insists that *all* of its employees work to their fullest potential. When one or more members of an organization are incapable or unwilling to put forth a top effort, and you're one of the top performers, you're going to wonder why you're busting your hump when the slackers are getting by with sub-standard output. If it keeps up, your attitude to management and the job will suffer, and so will your performance.

High recruiting costs: Recruiting is an expensive activity, especially for middle and higher level jobs as well as jobs of a highly technical nature such as scientists and engineers. Companies retain outside recruiters for such concentrated searches which cost thousands of dollars. Smaller companies may struggle to find the necessary money.

CHAPTER THREE
HIRING RISKS INHERENT
IN TODAY'S ECONOMY

The marketplace today is flooded with unemployed workers, most of them desperate to find employment . . . any employment. Indeed, McDonald's ran a national hiring day in spring, 2011 to find 50,000 able workers. An estimated one million applicants applied and the company filled the vacant jobs in a matter of hours. The media reported instances of applicants jostling, even fighting, one another for places in line.

You have to ask the question "How much attention could McDonald's management possibly focus on selecting the best applicants for the openings given the mass of applicants who applied and the air of desperation that hung over the hiring events? Mass hiring is simply not conducive to low turnover.

While high turnover may be the accepted norm in the fast food business that attracts teenage workers, it is not the accepted norm in other businesses where workers are responsible adults holding down jobs to support themselves and their families.

And that's the core of the problem. Since the 2008 market crash—and many economists would argue for many years before—the market has been inundated with unemployed workers. Any job opening immediately attracts a flood of applicants, no matter how menial the job. People today are understandably worried. Even the lowest paying job can spell the difference between people living in their homes or living on the street.

Under these burdensome circumstances how can an organization hire the very best when it has to sort through hundreds if not thousands of applications for job openings? Let's find out.

Marco Z. Ultimately Succeeds Using "Hire for Life" Principles

Remember Marco from Chapter One, the supervisor who almost lost his job because he was hiring marginal performers? He eventually learned the underlying principles of "Hire for Life" and dramatically improved his ability to select outstanding job candidates by applying certain core principles (you'll learn these in succeeding chapters). He came to realize that successful hiring and retention of employees is the key to both his success and the success of his organization. When his boss climbed aboard, the entire organization really started to hum.

Introducing the GAS Gauge (A Unique Way to Assess Job Candidates)

Marco also discovered the value of using the GAS Gauge, a method developed by Dean Hohl to assess the capability and staying power of job candidates. The GAS Gauge is a structured approach that helps the hiring manager evaluate any job candidate's (1) self-motivation and focus on organizational success, (2) unique strengths and abilities, and (3) growth potential. You'll learn more about the GAS Gauge and how to apply it in Chapter Nine, and watch it in action in Chapter Eleven.

It's been three years since Marco became a lifelong advocate of "Hire for Life" principles using GAS Gauge methodology; three years that witnessed a dramatic improvement in his department's productivity and quality. Here he is discussing "Hire for Life" principals with Jack, another supervisor in his company.

Jack is caught between the old school and new school of thinking. He was trained by old school supervisors (the "throw them in the water and let them swim" school). Part of the old way stuck, but Jack is comparatively new to supervision and searching for new ways to do his job better. He's just unsure what to do. You'll detect the ambivalence in his thinking from the following conversation as Marco coaches him:

"Marco, I don't understand why this is such a big deal. I mean just hire people who have the kind of experience needed for the job vacancy."

Marco smiles. "Then how come you terminated the last person you hired before his ninety-day probation was up?"

Jack clears his throat and looks away.

"And how come your department's productivity didn't improve last year?"

Jack blushes. "I see what you mean. . . . Okay, tell me where I'm going wrong, Marco."

"Thanks for your willingness to accept constructive advice, Jack. The bottom line is if you lower your standards you can fill every job in your department in a matter of hours. Just accept the first marginally acceptable job candidate who walks through the door. It's that simple and the results can be disastrous."

Jack nods. "I see your point. The market is flooded with unfortunate former employees who didn't make the cut. Many of those are marginal employees."

"The flip side," Marco says, "is the cost of vacant roles. Salespeople, for example. Without sales a company doesn't generate revenue. How long can a company afford to keep those kinds of jobs open? There's a lot of pressure to fill them quickly."

Jack thinks about that for a minute. "I guess those jobs take a lot of planning and preparation to make sure you're ready when somebody quits or gets promoted."

"Bingo! Part of the key to "Hire for Life" is developing specifications for new hires and selecting recruiting channels before the need arises, as well as planning backup for every position in the organization. Incidentally, that means *every new hire, not just key positions,* but truth be told some positions are harder to fill than others, so you'll need a contingency plan for those select jobs. Another way to say the same thing: Never lower your standards for any job opening or you'll fail on the 'business battlefield,' and be ready to recruit when vacancies occur. Don't get caught short."

"How about the recruiting side, Marco? Does everybody involved know what they're looking for?"

Marco slaps his knee. "You're catching on fast, Jack. Everybody—the outside recruiter you contract with to find new hires, your company's human resources recruiter, and the hiring managers in your company—all have to be on the same page. They must know ahead of time *exactly* what qualifications and experience new hires need, and they must all flawlessly execute their assignments to avoid hiring marginal or poor employees."

Jack nods. "I think I'm catching on. Preparation is the name of the game."

"Exactly. If the hiring process were perfect we'd never have the 80/20 rule at work. That's where 20 percent of a company's employees handle 80 percent of the workload. Our goal as supervisors and managers is to get to the 100 percent rule . . ."

"Let me guess. The rule where every employee carries his or her share of the workload, so you have 100 percent of employees   on   top   of   their   jobs."

"You got it. In that case, an organization can achieve miracles and produce the work of many more than its actual number of employees. That's the definition of synergism, by the way, where for example two employees working together produce the output of three employees. "Hire for Life" is a powerful dynamic."

"You've got a convert here."

Marco slaps Jack on the back. "Good for you. And don't forget, when filling vacant roles in your organization, think long term. Think ahead like the Rangers and keep your standards high. Don't settle. Don't compromise your standards. Lead the way on the 'business battlefield.' I'll show you a little later how a very simple but powerhouse technique called the GAS Gauge can help you achieve your goal."

"Hire for Life": The Hiring Equivalent of Zero Defects

In the eighties zero defects programs were the rage in manufacturing and supply chain businesses. They embraced the concept that producing defect-free products and services was not only possible, but near achievable (in the sense of reducing defective products from typical ranges of five to ten percent to a sustainable level of one-tenth of one percent). Companies that adopted the concept experienced dramatic improvements in quality and customer satisfaction.

"Hire for Life" is the application of zero defects to the hiring process. It states that it is possible to hire the best possible candidates and hold onto them throughout their working careers.

Use the following thoughts to formulate your zero defects ("Hire for Life") program:

- Every organization needs talented employees to grow.
- Key roles that are vacant have (lost) opportunity costs associated with them. Take great pains to assure that you plan ahead so you can "Hire for Life" in these positions and keep vacancies of key positions low, if non-existent.
- No winning organization can afford hiring the wrong employees on today's "business battlefield." Mistakes undermine the success of your organization.
- Turnover is hard to quantify but it's still co$tly!

- You'll never bat 1000 in hiring but you will improve your success rate with a methodology called GAS. You'll learn what GAS is and how to apply it in Chapter Nine. It's the hiring equivalent of zero defects.
- Take a long term view. Treat hiring as a return-on-investment (ROI) activity. Make *get it right the first time* your "Hire for Life" motto.

PART TWO

WINNING WITH THE
"HIRE FOR LIFE" ORGANIZATION

CHAPTER FOUR
GREAT EXPECTATIONS

Let's start with the basic hiring principles I learned in Ranger School. First, to be elite you have to keep high standards and never apologize for holding them. I'm advising you to apply those high standards as a *minimum requirement* for hiring in your organization.

For example, not everyone that made it through Army basic training passed jump school, and not everyone that passed with five jumps made it through the Ranger Indoctrination Program (RIP). Of those who made it to their Ranger units, many still couldn't uphold the Ranger Creed and high physical and mental demands required to become part of the elite special operations teams. Those who couldn't were consequently "terminated" from the Rangers, and sent to other regular Army units.

We had a saying that even those released from the Ranger battalion were often the very best regular Army unit soldiers.

This is an important principle: Just because they couldn't play "varsity" didn't mean those soldiers were bad. *But had we lowered our standards we wouldn't be as effective on the battlefield, during a raid, or airborne assault.* If you want to be the very best you have to maintain high standards and have Great Expectations. Never settle for anything less.

Often our Ranger platoons were staffed at 80 percent strength. We never operated with full strength teams. If a newbie joined the squad and he couldn't cut it, the rest of us just divvied up the load or responsibilities among fewer Rangers. Simply put, everyone had to work harder. You *never* lowered your standards just to fill a position. In combat that could cost you your life! On the 'business battlefield' it could cause your organization to fail. A result that would make your competitors jump with joy.

Rules of the Road

Let's further define and explain the concept of Great Expectations.

Rule #1 *If you want a winning team you must hire the best.* No exceptions. The minute you settle for second best or the minute you allow deviances from the type of person you want to hire, you're in trouble. More often than not you'll wind up with the type of failures Marco encountered. At best you'll achieve "average" performance. But "average" performance doesn't cut it in today's cutthroat business world where companies are failing right and left.

Rule #2 *Understand that not every job candidate you interview is cut out to become a member of your elite team.* I use the word "elite" deliberately. Just as in the example I described above (Army regular unit to jump school to Ranger battalion) very few will survive the cut. Accept the fact that you will have to screen and interview many job candidates to get to that one exceptional employee, but it's well worth the effort. Otherwise you'll shuffle endless numbers of employees through the mill and that's expensive and demoralizing and unnecessary. This rule carries two corollaries:

A. Just because a job candidate doesn't make it through your interviewing process to become a member of your team doesn't mean he or she is a bad person. That person is simply a bad fit. Just as with the Ranger example, most of these rejected candidates will move on to successful careers with other organizations.

B. Your selection process is not personal so don't make it personal. When you allow it to become personal, emotional considerations displace objective criteria, and that's when you lose sight of your goal: "Hire for Life."

Rule #3 *Don't feel guilty for having high standards, and certainly never apologize for them.* The managers and supervisors who should feel guilty are those who shortchange their organizations by hiring employees who (1) have less than sterling qualifications, and (2) may not be around a year or two down the road after their organizations have invested substantial dollars training and developing them. There can be no greater disappointment than organizational efforts that go awry because of hiring the wrong employees.

Rule #4 *Don't ever lower the bar just to fill a job.* If your organization doesn't have enough available talent, then do as the Rangers do; make do with what you have. Ask existing employees to shoulder the load until you have found that one single "right" employee that will help your organization excel at achieving its goals. The make-do employee will do just that: make do, and that's never enough in today's fiercely competitive environment. Believe your competitor has the same goal of hiring only the best. If that's true— and the very nature of competition says it is—if you lower the bar your competitors are going to beat you in corporate combat.

Rule #5 *When you "Hire for Life" treat the relationship between the organization and the new hire as a marriage.* Expect fidelity and it will be returned. Treat your new hire casually and you can expect something less than full-fledged commitment in return. And, please, no pre-nuptials (in this case contracts specifying monies and benefits paid in the event of a parting of the ways).

26

That's equivalent to planning for failure of the relationship. If you plan for failure, it's probably going to happen. The only way to assure hiring for life is to have a strong unbreakable bond between organization and employee focused on the long term.

Rule #6. *Finally, make hiring for life a requirement in every part of your company, from top to bottom and in all entities and locations.* It makes little sense to "Hire for Life" in division A and not in Division B. Employees in Division B will feel like second-class citizens (and they will be) if you consider them not as important as employees in Division A. On the other hand, employees in Division A will wonder about their company's true commitment if the same "Hire for Life" principle is restricted to their decision. Too much is at risk to do this half-ass.

CHAPTER FIVE
THE COMPETITIVE ADVANTAGES
"HIRE FOR LIFE" PROVIDES

DEF Brass Lamps International[4] had flirted with bankruptcy. Its sales had been trending down for several years along with its reputation in the marketplace. Missed customer shipments had become the norm and the company, for the first time in its 50 year history, had been experiencing a wave of customer complaints unlike anything seen before.

The company's board of directors decided it was time to take steps... It hired a consulting firm to analyze its failings and recommend new courses of action.

Based on those recommendations the board fired its chief executive officer and hired a new one. With the help of the consulting company, the new CEO replaced old operational practices with new innovational practices, including a dramatically different hiring procedure aimed at finding the best qualified job candidates, with the object of retaining them for the balance of their working careers.

Beyond the implementation of these new practices, the CEO infused the organization with a progressive attitude that embraced the "Hire for Life" approach: Do it right, do it to the best of your ability, and constantly seek improvement. With "Hire for Life" employees in place, this became a reality. Of course, a few employees didn't fit the mold and left the company, but those were the exceptions.

---

[4] Not the company's real name.

Success didn't happen overnight, nor did it happen without a lot of thought and effort. Yes, there were rough spots; bumps in the road. Employees needed and received coaching to implement best practices. They had to change the way they do things—never an easy task, but certainly doable. And the company had to modify some practices that didn't produce desired results.

Then again nothing worthwhile comes free. There is always a price, but the payoff was huge. Within a few years DEF Brass Lamps International was back on its feet. Here are some of the benefits the company realized from applying "Hire for Life" principles:

The company experienced higher profits, lower costs, and improved customer satisfaction. These benefits are the end result of the "Hire for Life" process and the ones most desired. The advantage of hiring the very best, then keeping them onboard and investing in their training and development, pays dividends that keep on giving.

Morale was vastly improved. Before the turnaround, when the company's sales and profits were plummeting there was a lot of finger pointing, a great deal of unhappy employees, and the constant threat of bankruptcy that kept employees at all levels of the company constantly on edge. During this period the company lost several key employees who had bailed out in anticipation of a shutdown. When the new team took over and adopted "Hire for Life" principles and things started to improve, so did morale.

Teamwork became the standard. The operating keywords "everybody look out for himself or herself" once the norm, was replaced by teamwork and cooperation and 'everybody look out for everybody else.' Employees who seldom or never talked with each other except when absolutely necessary, began cooperating under the banner of "together we succeed, apart we fail." The best way to characterize the new cooperative effort is that everybody and every company function now seemed to "gel."

Experts flourished in an environment rewarding experience. Employees, from top to bottom of the company, in every job, built levels of expertise as their years on the job increased. In the former regime there was so much turnover that new employees had to start from scratch building their job knowledge. Every time an employee quit, the company lost that expertise. "Hire for Life" reversed that trend and it paid dividends.

The company's improved reputation attracted both investors and prime job candidates. Media outlets learned of the company's improvement and wrote and reported on it. DEF Brass Lamps International became famous in the local community and in investing circles. When the company went public, investors snapped up stock and bond issues. Job openings drew the best possible candidates for jobs ranging from workers to top executives. "A" players at competing companies vied to become company employees.

CHAPTER SIX
RECRUITING CHANNELS:
WHERE IT WORKS AND WHERE IT DOESN'T

Over the years both experts and pretenders have written volumes of words about preferred recruiting channels for organizations seeking job candidates. Most of those words have focused on headhunters (recruiters) and agencies (I'll explain the difference in the following paragraphs), print ads, and online job boards such as Monster.com. In more recent years a lot of attention has focused on social networking websites Facebook and Linkedin and others like them. Few recruiting professionals, however, mention the power of referrals from fellow employees and trusted associates, frequently a more rewarding approach. We're going to discuss each recruiting channel in turn so you have the opportunity to choose the one or ones that suit your organization best.

Defining the "Right" Job Candidate

We are now entering the world of RASI (Recruiting, Assessing, Selecting, and Interviewing), critical steps in the "Hire for Life" process. Before it can begin, the hiring manager and Human Resources representative determine what attributes and experience the "right" candidate will possess. This is a critical step that narrows the search parameters for the recruiting channel and carries forward through assessment, selection, and interviewing until the hiring manager makes the final choice regarding which job candidate receives a job offer.

The danger with defining the "right" person too closely is that it may be impossible to fill the job opening because there has never been a "perfect" job candidate. The trick is to define the type of person you're seeking, stick to high standards, but don't restrict it so much you disqualify high performers. In other words, keep it real.

Once you've defined the "right" candidate, it's time to choose the recruiting channels.

Recruiters and Headhunters: The Good, the Bad, and the Ugly

Both retained recruiters and contingency recruiters are called headhunters. Companies pay retained recruiters a fee to find job candidates, even when recruiters don't fill the openings. (How long do you think companies will retain recruiters who don't produce results?) Companies pay contingency recruiters only when they fill jobs.

Contingency recruiters have the reputation of cutting corners. There have been instances of unscrupulous contingency recruiters throwing every available warm body at the hiring company in the fervent hope that one of them will get an offer. Unfortunately, this happens enough to damage the reputation of all recruiters.

The distinction between the two types of recruiters often blurs. There are honest and reliable contingency recruiters as well as ineffective and dishonest retained recruiters. The problem is finding a recruiter of any stripe you want to stick with, because over time that recruiter will come to understand your requirements and company culture so well he'll be able to select the best possible candidates for you. Here, as with hiring employees, "Hire for Life" rules.

Recruiters spare you the job of screening masses of resumes; the best recruiters will present you with three or four viable job candidates for a job opening. The main disadvantage is cost. Recruiters will charge in the neighborhood of 20 to 25 percent of the recruited job candidate's annual salary. A typical low to mid level supervisor making $40,000 would cost his company $8000 to $10,000. A lot of money. It's possible to have an arrangement with a recruiter that substantially lowers the fee if you assign the recruiter multiple searches.

The Problem with Traditional Print Ads

Let's face it. When you run an ad in the newspaper or in a magazine or online, chances are you're going to be flooded with responses, and many will be from left field. I've seen an ad for experienced production supervisors bring in resumes from a barber, a retail sales clerk, a casket salesman, even a Methodist minister. Sorting through the hundreds, if not thousands, of job applicants who respond to the ad is a daunting, frustrating task. It takes somebody accustomed to plowing through mountains of details (not everybody is cut out for this), and trying to sort through resumes and letters until they identify a handful of promising applicants.

As the hiring authority you can zero in a little more closely by stating specific job requirements and running the ad in specialized publications such as the *Wall Street Journal*. But it's still a crap shoot. Plan on spending a lot of time until you winnow it down to the three or four most promising candidates.

Online Job Boards

Indeed.com, now the largest job board of all, and Monster.com, the second largest, are but two examples of the increasing popularity of companies seeking job candidates and job candidates seeking companies online. These giants list hundreds of thousands of job openings along with millions of resumes. Other online job boards like Ladders focus on higher paying jobs with a $100,000 floor.

Companies seeking job candidates through online job boards have the advantage of filtering to select the types of employees they want without identifying their company identities. The disadvantage, as with responses to print ads, is that resumes tell only part of the story. The process is just beginning, but at least companies can pick and choose from what's available online.

Social Networking Websites

More and more companies are using social networking websites like Facebook to locate viable job candidates. There are literally dozens of such websites, some of them like Linkedin and Ning, devoted exclusively to business contacts.

Besides their search tool application, the social networking websites and instruments such as Google search can uncover much additional information about potential job candidates. It pays to research the applicants you're considering; it will provide an in-depth glimpse of their characters and personalities.

Referrals

The employees of your company as well as trusted business and social contacts often know outstanding potential employees working for other companies who might entertain the offer for a compelling opportunity. Referrals are mostly used for top level jobs but are just as applicable for any job opening in the company, from top to bottom. The object is to locate top notch people, and who better than the employees of your company and others who understand the "Hire for Life" model.

What's Best for You?

There isn't any right answer. What works for you may not work for others. For example, I know managers who have relied on recruiters with good results, others who run print ads or sort through online job boards and have savvy professionals in their human resources department screen resumes. Increasingly today, many search the social networking websites for talent. More and more companies are now using referrals to form the heart of their search.

At one time or another, companies resort to all of the recruiting channels just described. The choice is yours. Whichever you choose, it has to produce the type of job candidates that fit the "Hire for Life" profile you desire. If any major expense is involved it has to be cost effective.

CHAPTER SEVEN
ASSESSING JOB CANDIDATES

Here's the core of the job candidate assessment problem: You're experienced at your job, and you know how to interview and evaluate a job candidate's credentials. You think you can answer the four key questions that spell success or failure of an applicant with your company:

Does this candidate have the necessary qualifications for the job and growth potential to handle greater responsibilities?

Is the candidate motivated to succeed?

Will the candidate be a good fit for your organization's culture?

Does the candidate have the staying power needed to commit to a long term relationship with your company?

Unfortunately, if you're like most of us, your batting average as a hiring manager is not unblemished. You're right most of the time—job candidates you placed in your organization have worked out except for a couple of glaring errors. One where the candidate, a smooth talker, lied about his capabilities as a salesperson and you failed to uncover it until he didn't meet his sales goal for his territory for the year. Of course, you fired him.

In another instance the woman you hired as cost accounting manager turned out to be a marginal employee. Not enough to let her go, but enough where she has dragged down the performance of her section and you're now in the embarrassing position of letting upper management know you have to replace her.

Your batting average is 650, placing it in the great category for baseball but commonplace for business. As a result, your organization is performing well enough to stay in business, but your main competitor is cleaning your clock. You realize you must play catch up.

Wherein lies the problem?

Most supervisors and managers over time learn the mechanics of RASI (Recruiting, Assessing, Selecting, and Interviewing). But their hiring decisions are often highly subjective, a reflection of their personal experiences, and those experiences make it difficult to render an objective decision.

Your gut may tell you this is the right or wrong candidate for the job. That's not enough; you don't want to bat 650, you want to bat close to 1000. You need your gut feeling confirmed or denied by a more objective test. Third party assessment tools help add an objective element to the process and may shed light on the "real" candidate.

Third Party Assessment Tools

There are so many assessment tools it's difficult to know where to begin. So instead of listing the dozens of individual assessment tools available, let's categorize the more common of them.

Employee background checks. What's more fundamental than verifying a job candidate's record? This can be as simple as calling the job candidate's former employers and educational institutions. Or you can hire an outside agency to check everything about the job candidate including his credit record and military service.

Aptitude tests. These test a job candidate's ability to handle the work required by the job opening. Unlike a skills test (see below), aptitude tests measure the job candidate's ability to be trained to handle the position applied for.

Skills tests. Closely related to aptitude tests are those that evaluate an applicant's potential to be successful in her new position. This type of test has high marks in predicting how much on-the-job training the new hire will require. An offshoot of this are *job knowledge tests* that focus on job knowledge and technical expertise.

Personality tests. These tests measure the job candidate's personality traits needed to be successful for the job opening. You don't, for example, want to hire an introverted loner for a salesman's position. The tests evaluate such personality attributes and issues. There are a variety of personality tests, each proponent claiming her tests are superior to other tests. Defining which tests suit you best takes some thought.

Cognitive tests. An assessment of how well the job candidate thinks. It examines problem solving ability, reading comprehension, memory retention, perception, and reasoning.

Integrity tests. The job candidate's answers project his integrity or potentially devious behavior. The test's aim is to predict how honest and trustworthy the candidate may or may not be as a member of your organization.

Emotional maturity tests. The more contact a new hire has with others the more important her emotional maturity. Certainly, a supervisor's teamwork and social interaction skills are going to be more important than those of an engineer sitting at a drafting board all day.

Simulations. This involves creating a test environment where the job candidate performs tasks common to what the job opening demands while experts monitor his actions.

What's Best for You?

What tests should you use? That's something you have to determine for yourself, frequently by trial and error. The important lesson is that you need to balance your gut check with as many third party assessments as possible, given the restraints of time and money.

You're not going to bat 1000 about the right "Hire for Life" job candidates, but you can come close. The days of batting 650 are coming to an end because your competitors are improving their batting averages, too.

CHAPTER EIGHT
SELECTING AND INTERVIEWING
JOB CANDIDATES

The Selection Process

The selection process involves winnowing the available pool of job candidates until the company selects the final person to fill the job opening. In a graphic sense it's an inverted triangle, where the base of the triangle represents the number of people who applied for the job (in today's economy hundreds, possibly more) and the peak of the triangle which represents the applicant selected.

The GHI Advertising Agency,[5] a large advertising agency in the Southeast, ran an ad both online and in a local newspaper, advertising for a salesperson. Here is a snapshot of what its selection process looked like:

Selection Process Steps	Number of Candidates Left
Resumes and letters received in response to the ad	710
Human Resources (HR) culls resumes/letters into two piles: one for a further look, the other for the reject file.	203
HR makes a second review and cut	49

---

[5] Not the company's real name

HR conducts preliminary telephone interviews	10
Hiring manager makes his cut based on HR recommendations and reference check	4
On-site HR and hiring manager interviews of four candidates resulting in further winnowing	2
Job offer made	1

At the stage when the company had reduced the search to two viable job candidates, it subjected them to third party assessments. The number of assessments (three in this case: background verification, personality test, and business simulation) were based on how comfortable the hiring manager felt with his original gut feelings of the job candidates. If at any stage the assessments did not confirm his original feelings he had the option to either reject the candidates or subject them to further assessments. (He didn't.)

Cost usually plays a key role because third party assessments can be expensive. However, the hiring manager must weigh the cost of the assessments against the vastly larger cost of hiring employees who don't measure up to the company's expectations. In this example, the cost of the three tests were relatively expensive but the vice president of sales felt they were each important and his boss concurred.

The menu of assessments exposed a weakness in one of the job candidates that eliminated him from the competition, and GHI offered the salesman's job to the remaining candidate who accepted.

Interviewing Procedure

One of the strengths of the advertising agency's interviewing procedure was that seven of the company's managers and salespeople individually interviewed the final four applicants and compared notes after the interviews concluded. Each manager and salesperson was given the same set of questions to ask the applicants and was asked to phrase them differently.

The value of multiple interviews is that it brings different perspectives from (in this case) seven different managers and salespeople, which reveals strengths and weaknesses of the applicants the hiring manager may have missed. This process alone eliminated two of the four applicants.

These are the sort of answers the hiring manager was seeking:

Did all seven interviewers get the same answers to the same questions, albeit phrased differently?

Did they all have the same or similar impressions of the applicants and their ability to handle the sales job?

How did the applicants define top performance?

How able were the applicants to interpret problems and arrive at workable solutions?

The advertising agency at one time had conducted group interviews (seven managers together in the same room, with one manager after another, throwing questions at the applicant seated before them). The purpose was to see how well the applicants handled pressure. The company abandoned that approach because it was a false environment since any intelligent applicant would have prepared for this situation well in advance, thereby defeating the purpose of the group "interrogation."

Another facet of the advertising agency's hiring system involved postmortems to examine where the hiring process performed to expectations and where the hiring process failed. An extension of that same examination occurred whenever an employee quit or was terminated or demoted. Those events clearly signify a fault in the hiring process.

Hiring Process Cautions

A hiring manager can inadvertently compromise the hiring process. Pay attention to these cautions:

Infatuation. It's easy to become mesmerized by the bearing and eloquence of a smooth-talking job candidate. You admire how his suit fits, how unflappable he answers a battery of questions, how he conducts himself in a business-like manner. His behavior fairly shouts "great candidate." All of those qualities are admirable. What's not to like? Unfortunately, that infatuation clouds your judgment, and you stop probing for performance weaknesses. The applicant's appearance may mask serious faults in his staying power or his ability to get the job done. When you find your judgment clouded by surface factors pay particular attention to what other managers say about the candidate's ability. You may not be able to see clearly.

Trust but verify. You can never make enough checks, but you can always make too few. The purpose of many parties interviewing job candidates and subjecting them to third party assessments is to confirm or deny your original impressions.

Check references carefully . . . if you can. Ask the candidate's references and former bosses open-ended questions that may reveal the candidate's job effectiveness. In this day and age where job candidates routinely sue references that bad-mouth them, you may have to read between the lines. In some instances companies may provide employment dates and nothing else.

One way to evaluate the abilities and staying power of job candidates is the GAS method I've previously mentioned. We'll now examine it.

CHAPTER NINE
GAS GAUGE: THE HEART OF THE INTERVIEW

The RASI process (Recruiting, Assessing, Selecting, and Interviewing) describes the steps needed to identify and hire only the most capable employees and retain them throughout their careers. An organization composed of high performers with close to zero turnover is an organization that will excel and defeat competitive threats.

The GAS Gauge interviewing tool is at the heart of the interview. It's a structured approach aimed at uncovering candidates' strengths and weaknesses and helps you determine whether or not you want them on your team. GAS is composed of three elements:

G1...Give-A-Shit. Pardon the vernacular but I can think of no better way to express this element. Does the candidate really care about his organization's success? Does he have the prerequisite drive to succeed? Is he self-motivated or does he need jump starting? Will he be focused or reckless in his pursuit of goals?

G2...Great-@-Something. What sets this candidate apart from the rest of the field? Can your organization leverage her unique qualities, and will it give your organization a competitive advantage? How well will the candidate meld with the other members of the organization?

G3...Grow-&-Scale. Does the candidate have potential to grow and contribute to tomorrow's organization? How flexible is the candidate? How diverse are his skill sets, education, and experience? What do you see this candidate doing in your organization three to five years from now?

A well constructed resume will display at least one example of G1, G2, and G3. *If it doesn't don't schedule the interview.* Chances are this will not be the type of job candidate you're seeking. Assuming the resume contains at least one full GAS example, you can discover the rest during the face to face interview.

Let's examine each in turn to find out the types of probing questions that reveal how the candidate measures up to G1, G2, and G3.

G1: Give-A-Shit

Responses to the questions and requests for information in this category surface how well focused the candidate will be on his or her success and the success of the organization. Examples:

What's the biggest challenge in life you've had to face and how did you deal with it?

Would you do anything different if you had to do it over?

Tell us about a goal you really had to strive for. What were the results and were you truly satisfied with them?

What is the biggest setback you've had to overcome? How did you stay on course?

G2: Great-@-Something

Responses to the questions and requests for information in this category reveal the candidate's exceptional and unique qualities that make her stand out. Examples are:

What sets you apart from your peers?

Why are you the best candidate for this job?

What is your most outstanding attribute?

What is your greatest talent?

What do your peers compliment you on most?

G3: Grow-&-Scale

Responses to the questions and requests for information in this category demonstrate the candidate's ability to grow beyond his current job and make even larger future contributions to the organization. Examples are:

How do you stay on top of your field of expertise?

What was the shortest time between promotions at any of your previous employers? What was the longest? Provide examples for both and explain why.

What do you see yourself doing in three to five years?

What do you want to achieve professionally?

How would you handle it if the scope of your job doubled over the next couple of years?

The GAS Gauge

How do you apply and measure the GAS Gauge method? We'll use an example of a suture manufacturing company, JKL International[6], now seeking a production supervisor for its packaging line. The company's vice president of manufacturing has interviewed Paul, a twenty-three-year-old college graduate with two years experience in suture manufacturing. Paul is currently working for a competitor.

At the conclusion of Paul's interview, the vice president of manufacturing drew a graph plotting columns "A", "@", and "&" against three rows of examples (labeled E1, E2, and E3 on the top of the graph). The following page titled GAS Gauge Diagram for Paul shows the results.

GAS Gauge Diagram for Paul

	E1	E2	E3
"A"	On my own at 18, parents died. Worked my way through college.	Joined industry packaging group and chaired new products committee.	Investigated and found reasons for packaging seal problems that caused FDA concern. Worked on my own time with engineering to get a fix.
	Despite severe inherited union problems when	Developed new quality standards that helped our	Started packaging line for current employer,

---

6 Not the company's real name.

"@"	I became supervisor I worked with union members and union officials over a period of two years to restore our management-union relationship. HR now asks my help to solve knotty union problems.	packaging stand out against competitors.	including writing its standard operating procedures.
"&"	Working on duel master's degree in package engineering and business.	Company assigned me additional responsibilities of supervising another sub-assembly line after six months on the job.	At work the company accepted me for its middle management training program.

To reiterate a point I made before, do not invite a job candidate in for an interview if you can't complete at least one GAS column (E1 for G1, G2, and G3 completely).

CHAPTER TEN
ASSIMILATION, ADAPTATION,
AND ADVANCEMENT

"Hire for Life" the Ranger way does not stop once the new hire is aboard. There are still a few important steps needed (1) to assure that he or she fits well within and is accepted by the organization, and (2) to conduct a postmortem and tweak the hiring process to neutralize weaknesses and strengthen its ability to "Hire for Life."

Once the new hire is aboard you need to make sure the transition process is successful. This process, also known as onboarding, protects your investment in employees so it continues to provide returns for years to come. Here are typical steps:

Assign an experienced employee to guide the new hire and introduce her to the organization.

Introduce the new hire to employees within her section and to other functions and their employees so she understands the role her section plays in the overall organization.

Help the new hire understand the culture of the company. Learning about the organization's successes and failures from fellow employees helps orient her.

Understand that with every new hire the organization changes, perhaps slightly, perhaps significantly. Astute managers take this into account when making and executing plans. Clearly define the responsibilities of each employee to avoid confusion and frustration.

Place the new hire in a section that has a manager capable of being a mentor and role model. Time after time I have seen young, inexperienced new hires placed under the direction of managers with poor, if not bad, attitudes. Enough exposure to such bad eggs ruins new employees eager to make good. (Ask yourself why you continue to tolerate such managers, anyway.)

Invest in the new hire in the form of training and development. Be conscious of the new hire's potential as well as the contribution she can make today.

Follow-up on the new hire's progress. Like anything else, without adequate checks something slips between the cracks.

Next Steps

To keep the "Hire for Life" process from deteriorating you need to conduct periodic checks of how well the process is working. Your first step will be to perform a gap analysis to address the ineffective areas of the process and capitalize on best practices for fixes.

A perfect time for this postmortem is (1) after you have hired a new employee and (2) every time you fire or demote an employee or when an employee quits. In the former case you will be trying to reinforce what you did right, and in the latter case discovering what you did wrong and correcting it. This constant tweaking assures that your "Hire for Life" process will continue functioning at a high level of achievement.

You should use the information from your gap analysis to educate the recruiting team. Like the rest of your organization, they need constant reinforcement to remind them of where the "Hire for Life" process succeeded and where it broke down and what they can do to correct weak or ineffective practices.

The same goes for your hiring managers and decision makers. They, too, function as integral components of the team and need continuing direction.

CHAPTER ELEVEN
MARCO Z. GETS PROMOTED:
ANATOMY OF A "HIRE FOR LIFE" SUCCESS STORY

Remember Marco Z. from Chapter Three? His successful adoption of "Hire for Life" principles and use of the GAS Gauge to assess the drive, strengths, and capabilities of job candidates resulted in his promotion to production superintendant.

What follows are the steps Marco took to assure that whoever replaced him was the absolute best candidate for the job. This structured approach will help you when it comes time to select a candidate to fill a job opening in your organization:

Step 1: Examine the job to see if it has changed.

Marco decided to re-evaluate the demands of his former job of supervisor, recognizing that over time things change, and often those changes are so gradual that in the heat of everyday battle, it's all too common to miss their impact on operations.

Once he stepped back from the job he noticed things he hadn't seen before. For example, when Marco was first promoted to supervisor over three years before, his department's tooling requirements were fairly primitive. But over the past few years the company had developed new products that demanded more complex tools and fixtures and a supervisor with a technical background to understand them. He factored this change and others he found into the new job requirements.

Step 2: Develop specifications for the job.

This is a critical and sometimes overlooked step. It's all too easy to say that we need a new production supervisor, and let it go at that. Production managers know what a production supervisor is and what qualifications the job requires.

Or do they? Not only do job conditions change over the years as examined in Step 1 above, so do the demands on employees. Competition, both inside the company and in the marketplace, gets tougher and more stringent with each passing year. Every year you must bring in costs lower than the previous year; you must increase sales; you must improve quality to meet new and more demanding customer requirements; you must improve productivity; and so on. As we have seen in recent years, only smart and tough companies survive in such an environment. That means for every job opening *carefully and thoroughly* analyzing job specifications, setting them down on paper, and having all those affected by the job opening discuss and sign off on the revised specifications. It takes a lot of introspection and a lot of leg work, but the end result is well worth it.

Consulting with supervisors and workers in his department and the human resources manager Marco developed new job specifications for the supervisory opening. Those fresh requirements, described in the written job specifications, were then reviewed and signed off by his boss (the vice president of manufacturing), relevant department heads, and the company president. It's just this kind of involvement that often spells the difference between success and failure in the hiring process. Nothing is as crucial to a company's longevity and profitability as hiring the right people. The executive team in Marco's company realized that.

Step 3: Prepare probing interview questions.

Next on the list is the step most frequently omitted by hiring managers: thinking out and preparing probing interview questions that expose the "true" job candidates, not the pretty pictures they present in interviews.

This step is choreographed. It plans who is going to ask what questions and when and in what context. In Marco's case the interviewers were Marco himself, the HR manager, Marco's boss (the vice president of manufacturing), the manager of engineering, and the manager of production planning and control. All five managers were instructed to work from the same interview form but phrase their questions differently, not only to reveal deception, but also to expose different aspects of the job candidate's background.

Step 4: Recruit and select candidates.

It is the policy of Marco's company to promote from within whenever possible. Marco and his boss put their heads together and came up with the names of three outstanding internal candidates: two workers from Marco's department and one worker from another department.

Marco decided to add two outside job candidates to the mix. He asked the human resources manager to get referrals from employees. The HR manager canvassed the company's best employees (on the assumption that successful people with the same work ethic stick together) and came up with four names. She asked the referring employees to sound out the interest of their suggested candidates. Three of them, all working elsewhere expressed an interest in the company and submitted resumes. The HR manager checked their references, telephone interviewed them, and narrowed the choices to two outside candidates. With Marco's help she constructed GAS Gauge diagrams for both outside candidates and all three inside candidates. She then asked the two outsiders to come in for face to face interviews. The pool of job candidates now rose to five.

Marco and the HR manager decided that all five were viable (but not yet vetted) candidates for the job and they would need no others. This, of course, is an ideal condition. In many, if not most, job searches the company would have been forced to sift through dozens if not hundreds of resumes from recruiters, job ads in the newspapers or online job boards to narrow the search to a viable few.

Step 5: Appraise the candidate pool.

The interviews for the five candidates were scheduled separately but within the same week. This proximity allowed interviewers to make comparisons while the interviews were still fresh in their minds.

The five interviewing managers met, discussed, and compared all five candidates and reviewed their GAS Gauge diagrams. From this evaluation the field was narrowed to the best two job candidates: one an employee, the other an outsider. Everyone agreed that the finalists represented the type of people they wanted to work for the company. But just to make sure, Marco and the HR manager decided to conduct a background investigation of the two finalists and subject them to tests of personality, leadership style, emotional stability, and cognitive abilities, administered by an independent organizational development specialist.

Step 6: Make the final decision.

For the final selection, Marco, his boss (the vice president of manufacturing) and company president interviewed the two finalists again. After the interviews, Marco along with the president, vice president of manufacturing and HR manager made a final joint review of the finalists. The background check conducted by an outside agency included references, education achievements, employment dates, credit checks, military service records, and arrest records (neither had ever been arrested). Both candidates passed with flying colors.

The psychological assessment, however, told a different story.

The outside candidate had charmed every interviewer other than the vice president of manufacturing, who detected a little bit of a snow job. The interviewing psychologist with the independent testing company concurred. She questioned the outside candidate's sincerity. That was enough to rule him out. The remaining candidate, the inside employee, got the job.

Step 7: Conduct post-hire introductions, orientation and follow-up.

The executives at Marco's company understand the merit of investing in their employees. Once the new supervisor was aboard he spent the first two weeks in an orientation program that familiarized him with the company's different functions. Moreover, this gave him the opportunity to establish relationships with employees of those departments. In his own section he worked side-by-side for one day with each worker to get to know each better, find out his or her job skills and responsibilities, and gather ideas for improving operations.

Marco closely monitored the new supervisor's progress. He made it a point to be alert to any of his problems (as he was with the other supervisors reporting to him). Marco wisely considered that an essential part of his job was to remove roadblocks so his direct reports could function smoothly and according to plan.

For the first year, Marco conducted monthly reviews with the new supervisor to tweak his performance and provide him a chance to discuss both departmental problems and opportunities for improvement. In this fashion he gave his new supervisor a strong foundation.

CHAPTER TWELVE
SUMMARY

At the core of the "Hire for Life" process are two key elements: RASI and the GAS Gauge. Let's review them.

Focus on the RASI process

The points below are the essence of your RASI process:

Great Expectations: Understand the job requirements and keep your expectations high.

The cost of vacant roles: Know the cost of vacant roles, especially those for key jobs and plan ahead so you don't get caught short.

The cost of hiring marginal employees. If you do get caught short (unanticipated events such as a sudden death), do not compromise and hire anybody less than a high performer. Marginal employees defeat the purpose of the "Hire for Life" process and will eventually drag down your organization.

Follow the RASI procedure. It's constructed to filter through dozens, if not hundreds, of aspiring job candidates to arrive at the best possible choice.

Use GAS Gauge diagrams to narrow down the best candidates. Design questions that dig deeply into the candidate's capability and attitude.

Don't forget A3: assimilation, adaptation, and advancement. To make the new employee's transition successful takes careful thought and attention.

GAS Gauge questions

Questions asked by interviewers are at the core of the GAS Gauge. Without the right kind of questions, the GAS Gauge simply does not have the same impact as with them. Keep the following points in mind:

Create a pool of GAS Gauge questions unique to your organization and industry. Your interviewers such as hiring managers and human resources representatives can then operate from the same page. One of the real values of similarly worded GAS Gauge questions is to check the reliability of the candidates' answers when the interviewers compare notes.

Keep this list of questions updated and dynamic. Make the questions relevant and revealing. Open ended questions work best. Asking questions that candidates can answer with a perfunctory yes or no do nothing to reveal the candidates' true selves. Neither do leading questions that reveal the answer in the question itself, such as "What's more important, productivity or quality?" Any savvy interviewee will tell you both. If the candidate answers with a preference, that's an indication you shouldn't have asked him in for an interview to begin with.

Make your GAS Gauge questions as specific as possible and job related. From your post mortem, purge ineffective ones.

APPENDIX

Ready to Use GAS Gauge Diagram

	E1	E2	E3
"A"			
"@"			
"&"			